MATH IN MY WORLD

TELLING TIME
ALL THE TIME

By Jean Sharp

Reading consultant: Susan Nations, M.Ed.,
author/literacy coach/consultant in literacy development
Math consultant: Rhea Stewart, M.A., mathematics content specialist

WEEKLY READER®
PUBLISHING

Please visit our web site at www.garethstevens.com
For a free color catalog describing our list of high-quality books,
call 1-800-542-2595 (USA) or 1-800-387-3178 (Canada). Our fax: 1-877-542-2596

Library of Congress Cataloging-in-Publication Data

Sharp, Jean.
    Telling time all the time / Jean Sharp.
        p. cm. — (Math in our world. Level 2)
     ISBN-13: 978-0-8368-9001-3 (lib. bdg.)
     ISBN-10: 0-8368-9001-9 (lib. bdg.)
     ISBN-13: 978-0-8368-9010-5 (softcover)
     ISBN-10: 0-8368-9010-8 (softcover)
     1. Time—Juvenile literature. I. Title.
    QB209.5.S44 2008
    529—dc22   2007029086

This edition first published in 2008 by
Weekly Reader® Books
An Imprint of Gareth Stevens Publishing
1 Reader's Digest Road
Pleasantville, NY 10570-7000 USA

Copyright © 2008 by Gareth Stevens, Inc.

Senior Editor: Brian Fitzgerald
Creative Director: Lisa Donovan
Graphic designer: Alexandria Davis

Photo credits: cover & title page © Corbis; pp. 5, 22 © David Young-Wolff/PhotoEdit; p. 6
© Tom McCarthy/PhotoEdit; p. 7 © Ariel Skelley/Corbis; p. 8 © Christina Kennedy/PhotoEdit;
p. 9 © Will Hart/PhotoEdit; p. 11 © Robin Nelson/PhotoEdit ; p. 12 © Jeff Greenberg/PhotoEdit;
p. 13 © Tony Freeman/PhotoEdit; pp. 14, 19, 23 © Myrleen Ferguson Cate/PhotoEdit; p. 15 ©
Bob Daemmrich/PhotoEdit; pp. 17, 18 © Michael Newman/PhotoEdit; p. 21 © Spencer Grant/
PhotoEdit.

Printed in the United States

CPSIA Compliance Information: Batch # CR112050GS: For further information contact Gareth Stevens, New York, New York at 1-800-542-2595.

TABLE OF CONTENTS

Words that appear in the glossary are printed in **boldface** type the first time they occur in the text.

Chapter 1:
Morning

It is **morning.** The children on Park Street are busy. They have many things to do. What will they do this morning?

Jenn wakes up at 7:00 in the morning. It is time to get ready for school. She washes her face and brushes her teeth. She gets dressed for school.

Henry has breakfast with his family. They eat at 7:30 in the morning. They have cereal and fruit juice. Henry has milk to drink.

Kaya and his dad walk to the bus stop.
The bus comes at 8:00 every morning.
It takes the children to Park Street School.
They want to get to school on time.

The children arrive at school. The
school bell rings at 8:30 in the morning.
The children line up to go to class.

In the morning the children work at
centers. At 10:30 Jon and Devin work in
the math center. They practice math games.

Chapter 2:
Afternoon

It is **afternoon.** The children on Park Street are busy. They have many things to do. What will they do this afternoon?

The children have art class at 2:30 in the afternoon. Today they use crayons and paper to draw pictures.

The bell rings at 3:00 every afternoon. The children line up to go home. School is over for the day. The children have many things to do after school.

Some children play soccer after school. They play at the park near the school. Practice starts at 3:30. The children run and play with their friends.

Other children take music lessons after school. They practice their instruments. They work with the music teacher. Their lessons start at 3:30.

Many children do their homework after
school. Kim begins her homework at 4:00 in
the afternoon. She finishes her math. She and
some other children pick out books to read.

Chapter 3:
Evening

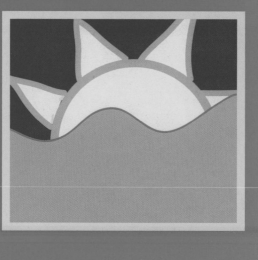

It is **evening.** The children on Park Street are busy. They have many things to do. What will they do this evening?

Chen has dinner with his family. He helps his father in the kitchen. Chen sets the table for dinner. They eat dinner at 6:00 in the evening.

6:30

Ben and his family go for an evening walk. They leave the house at 6:30. They walk around their neighborhood. It is good exercise for them!

At 7:00 Tony reads with his family. They read a story together every evening. Tony likes mystery stories. His little brother likes scary books.

Chapter 4:
Night

It is **night.** The children on Park Street
are busy. They have many things to do.
What will they do tonight?

Quinton gets ready for bed. He brushes
his teeth at 7:30 each night. He puts on his
pajamas and says good night to his family.

8:00

Ana picks out her clothes for the next
day. She gets into bed at 8:00 each night.
She listens to music before she goes to sleep.

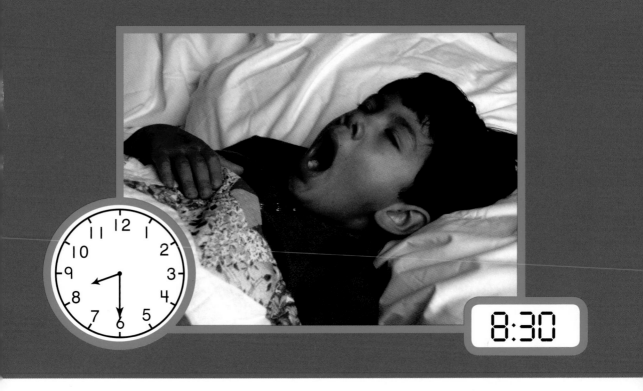

Josh goes to bed at 8:30 each night. His dad turns off the light in his room. "Good night. Tomorrow will be another busy day," says his dad.

Glossary

afternoon: the part of day between noon and sunset

evening: the end of the day between late afternoon and the first part of night

morning: the part of the day from sunrise until noon

night: the part of the day between sunset and sunrise

About the Author

Jean Sharp has written numerous books and educational software programs for children. She lives with her family in Minneapolis, Minnesota.